EXAMINING BACKYARD HABITATS

Zelda King

PowerKiDS press™

New York

Published in 2009 by The Rosen Publishing Group, Inc.
29 East 21st Street, New York, NY 10010

First Edition

Editor: Joanne Randolph
Book Design: Kate Laczynski
Photo Researcher: Jessica Gerweck

Photo Credits: Cover, pp. 1, 7 (desert), 19 (pears) © www.istockphoto.com; pp. 5, 9 (red squirrel, garter snake, milk snake, raccoon, red fox, skunk, American toad, red-spotted newt), 11, 13, 15 (stages 5 and 7), 17, 21 Shutterstock.com; p. 7 (mountain) © www.istockphoto.com/Nick Belton; p. 9 (bat) © www.istockphoto.com/ Torsten Stahlberg; p. 9 (deer mouse) © www.istockphoto.com/Katherine Garrenson; p. 9 (grey squirrel) © www.istockphoto.com/Roger Whiteway; p. 15 (stage 2) © www.istockphoto.com/Thomas Koellner; p. 15 (stage 3) © J&C Sohns/Age Fotostock; p. 15 (stage 4) © ARCO/R. Hicker/Age Fotostock; p. 19 (roses) © www.istockphoto.com/Amanda Rohde; p. 19 (blackberries) © www.istockphoto.com/Andrew Hyslop; p. 19 (clovers) © www.istockphoto.com/Carly Hennigan; p. 19 (pine) © www.istockphoto.com/Anders Aagesen; p. 19 (holly) © www.istockphoto.com/Ann Taylor-Hughes.

Library of Congress Cataloging-in-Publication Data

King, Zelda.
  Examining backyard habitats / Zelda King. — 1st ed.
     p. cm. — (Graphic organizers : Habitats)
  Includes index
  ISBN 978-1-4358-2720-2 (library binding) — ISBN 978-1-4358-3124-7 (pbk.)
  ISBN 978-1-4358-3130-8 (6-pack)
  1. Garden ecology—Juvenile literature. 2. Backyard gardens—Juvenile literature. 3. Habitat (Ecology)—
Juvenile literature. I. Title.
  QH541.5.G37K53 2009
  577.5′54—dc22
                              2008024314

Manufactured in the United States of America

CONTENTS

WHAT IS A BACKYARD HABITAT?

Earth has many habitats. They are the different places where plants and animals live. You may think that habitats are places far from where you live. Did you know that you can find one right outside your home, though? A backyard is a habitat!

Many plants and animals live in a backyard. A good way to learn about a backyard habitat is by using graphic organizers. You could start, for example, with a chart that lists all the plants and animals in your yard. You will find graphic organizers in this book that will teach you cool facts about a backyard habitat!

A backyard might have grass, some trees and bushes, flowers, and other plants. These make good homes for squirrels, bugs, snakes, and lots of other animals.

ALL SORTS OF BACKYARD HABITATS

A backyard is a backyard, right? This is not really true. The plants and animals found in a backyard are different in different places. Desert plants and animals are different from mountain plants and animals, for example. A city backyard is different from a rural, or country, backyard, too. What kind of backyard do you have at your house?

This book will talk about a rural backyard near a forest in the Northeast. Even if you live in a different kind of place, you will read about some plants and animals that you know. You will learn about some new ones, too!

This compare/contrast chart shows some of the animals that live in desert backyards and mountain backyards. Are there animals in this chart that are found in both places?

Compare/Contrast Chart: A Desert Backyard and a Mountain Backyard

	Desert Backyard Habitat	Mountain Backyard Habitat
Pine trees		X
Cactuses	X	
Woodpeckers	X	X
Northern pygmy owls		X
Elf owls	X	
Striped skunks		X
Snowshoe hares		X
Jackrabbits	X	
Raccoons		X
Squirrels	X	X
Mice	X	X
Least chipmunks		X
Kangaroo rats	X	
Toads	X	X
Horned lizards	X	
Wood frogs		X
Desert tortoises	X	

WHAT LIVES IN A BACKYARD HABITAT?

Many kinds of animals think a rural backyard near a northeastern forest is a perfect habitat. During the day, you will see lots of squirrels. You may also see chipmunks darting around. If you peer into tall grass, you might spot a **garter snake** or a **milk snake**.

A different group of animals appears at night. Red-spotted **newts** come out from under their rocks. Raccoons may appear. You may hear American toads calling loudly, even if you do not see them. A white-tailed deer might come to eat some plants. Look up, and you might see bats flying around!

This classifying web groups some day and night animals based on what animal family they belong to. Can you think of some backyard bugs and birds to add to the web?

Classifying Web: Animals in a Forest Backyard Habitat

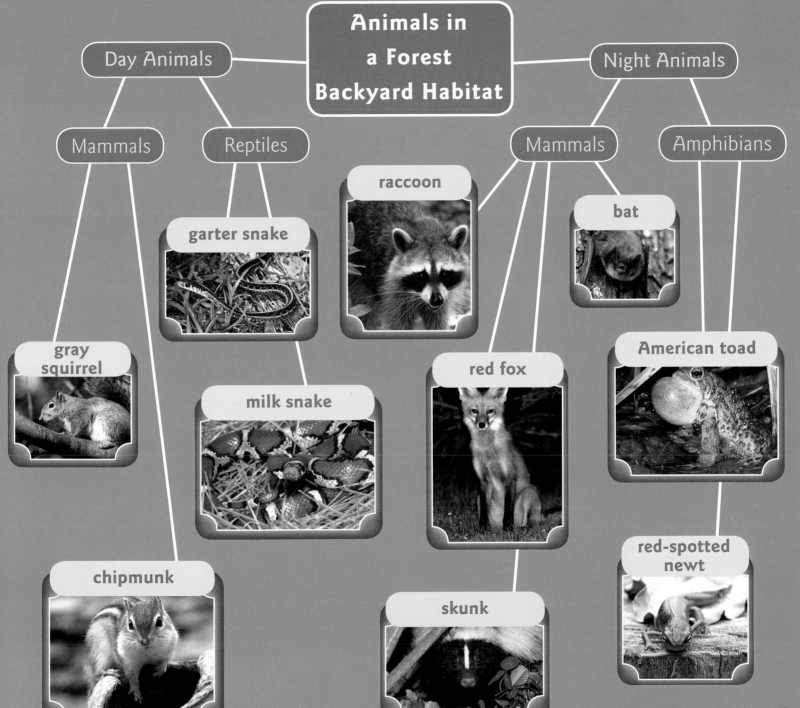

Animals in a Forest Backyard Habitat

Day Animals
- Mammals
  - gray squirrel
  - chipmunk
- Reptiles
  - garter snake
  - milk snake

Night Animals
- Mammals
  - raccoon
  - bat
  - red fox
  - skunk
- Amphibians
  - American toad
  - red-spotted newt

A CHIPMUNK IS ALWAYS BUSY

Chipmunks make a noise that sounds like "Chip! Chip! Chip!" This sound gave chipmunks their name. Chipmunks like to talk. In fact, they like to get together and sing sometimes!

In warm weather, chipmunks are always busy gathering seeds. They stuff the seeds into pouches in their cheeks. When their pouches are full, they race to their **burrows** to store the seeds. All the while, they watch for enemies. They rush away if they see one.

Most chipmunks live alone. Mothers and babies live together, though. Young chipmunks stay with their mothers for about seven weeks. Then they leave to make their own burrows.

Chipmunks are common in backyards near forests. This sequence chart shows the things that happen each year in a chipmunk's life.

Sequence Chart: A Chipmunk's Year

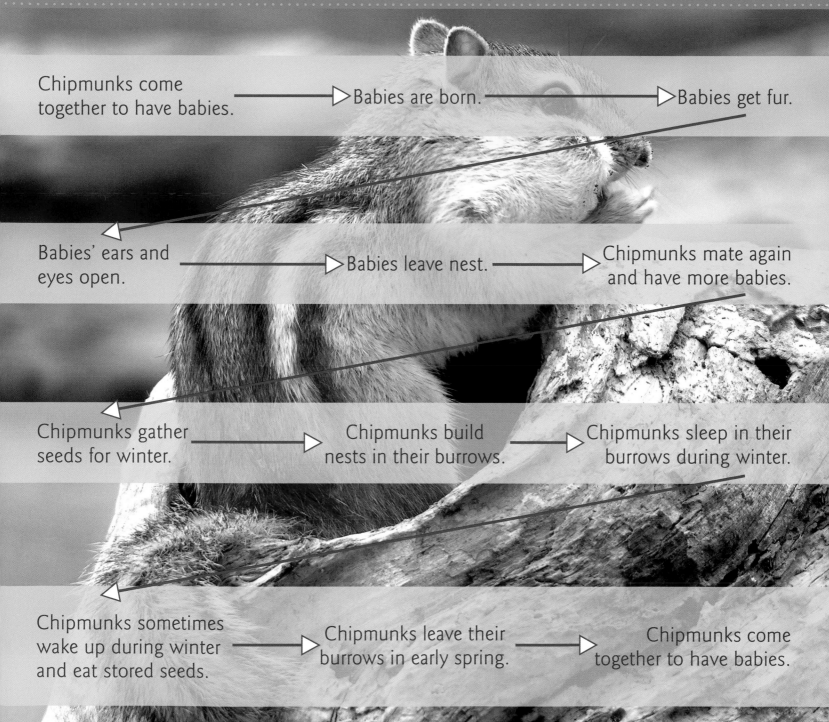

Chipmunks come together to have babies. ▷ Babies are born. ▷ Babies get fur.

Babies' ears and eyes open. ◁ ▷ Babies leave nest. ▷ Chipmunks mate again and have more babies.

Chipmunks gather seeds for winter. ◁ ▷ Chipmunks build nests in their burrows. ▷ Chipmunks sleep in their burrows during winter.

Chipmunks sometimes wake up during winter and eat stored seeds. ◁ ▷ Chipmunks leave their burrows in early spring. ▷ Chipmunks come together to have babies.

11

SO MANY BIRDS!

Many birds are part of a backyard habitat. Their singing fills the air in spring and summer.

You might see bright yellow **goldfinches**, **chickadees** with black caps, bright blue **indigo buntings**, and tiny hummingbirds. There are also robins, woodpeckers, blue jays, cardinals, and crows. Sometimes huge wild turkeys come! A red-tailed hawk may appear to hunt small birds and animals. At night, you might hear the call of an eastern screech owl.

Some birds stay all year. Others, such as robins and hummingbirds, **migrate** to warmer places in the fall and return in the spring.

This spider map shows some facts about four backyard birds. Can you find out which bird drills holes in trees to find food?

Spider Map: Backyard Birds

WOODPECKER

Eats mostly bugs living in trees

Long bill for drilling into trees

Strong feet and sharp claws to hang on to trees

CHICKADEE

Small

Eats bugs, seeds, nuts, and fruit

Often hangs upside down from tree branch

BACKYARD BIRDS

Small

Large, strong bills

Eats seeds

GOLDFINCH

Small

Hunts at night

Eats mice and bugs

OWL

WHAT IS THAT HUMMING SOUND?

Hummingbirds got their name because they make a humming sound. They do not make that sound with their beaks, though. They beat their wings so fast that they hum! Hummingbirds beat their wings more than 50 times each second!

Northeastern backyards have ruby-throated hummingbirds. They are about 4 inches (10 cm) long. They have bright green backs and white stomachs. Males have bright red throats. Females have white throats. They eat bugs and drink **nectar** from flowers.

Ruby-throated hummingbirds migrate in the fall. These tiny birds fly all the way to Mexico or Central America! That is where they spend the winter.

A cycle organizer is a great way to show steps that happen over and over. This organizer shows the life cycle of a hummingbird.

Cycle Organizer: A Ruby-Throated Hummingbird's Life Cycle

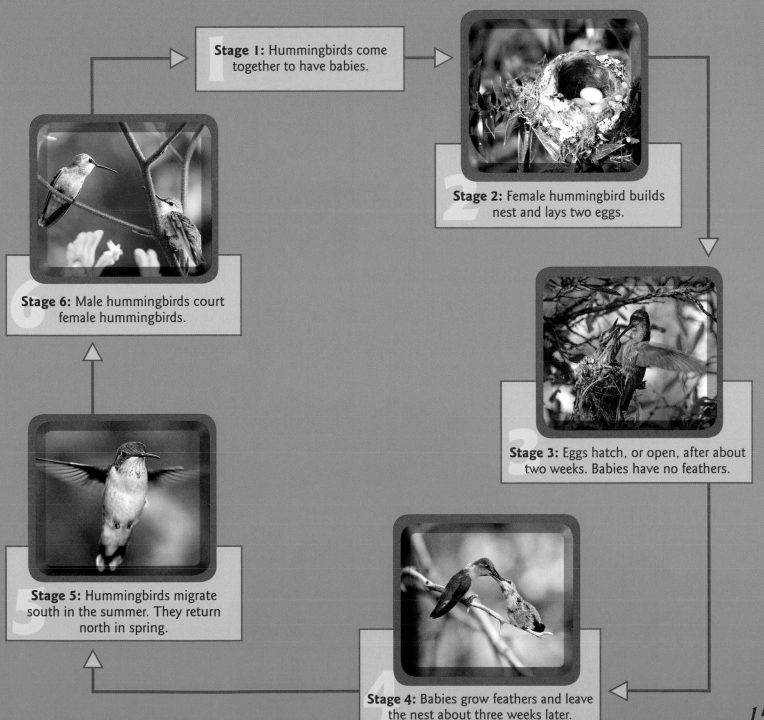

Stage 1: Hummingbirds come together to have babies.

Stage 2: Female hummingbird builds nest and lays two eggs.

Stage 3: Eggs hatch, or open, after about two weeks. Babies have no feathers.

Stage 4: Babies grow feathers and leave the nest about three weeks later.

Stage 5: Hummingbirds migrate south in the summer. They return north in spring.

Stage 6: Male hummingbirds court female hummingbirds.

15

BUGS ARE EVERYWHERE!

Did you know that a backyard has more bugs than any other animal? There are common flies and beautiful dragonflies, whose long, thin bodies may be red, green, or blue. You may see ladybugs on leaves. Tiger **swallowtail** butterflies, with yellow and black stripes, fly from flower to flower.

You may also see **carpenter** ants and carpenter bees. They are called carpenters because they tunnel in wood to make their homes.

Carpenter ants are night bugs. Beautiful, pale green luna moths and **mosquitoes** are as well. Female mosquitoes will bite you to get your blood. Luckily, bats like to eat mosquitoes!

Venn diagrams compare how things are alike and different. Can you find some ways that ladybugs, dragonflies, and mosquitoes are all the same?

Venn Diagram: Mosquito, Dragonfly, and Ladybug

MOSQUITO

- one pair of wings
- feelers used to hear and smell
- cannot open mouth
- has tubelike mouthpart used to sip plant juices and blood

MOSQUITO AND DRAGONFLY

- lay eggs in or near water

DRAGONFLY

- three life stages
- feelers used to tell how fast it is flying
- has mouthparts made for biting
- uses legs to catch food while flying
- can fly forward, backward, and hang in air

ALL

- three body parts
- two eyes
- two feelers
- three pairs of legs
- breathe through air holes in body

MOSQUITO AND LADYBUG

- four life stages

DRAGONFLY AND LADYBUG

- two pairs of wings
- eat bugs

LADYBUG

- feelers used to smell, taste, and feel
- has mouthparts made for chewing
- back pair of wings are hard and cover back wings when not flying
- lays eggs on leaves of land plants

WHAT GROWS IN A BACKYARD HABITAT?

All sorts of wild plants grow in a backyard in a rural forest area. You can find trees that stay green all year, such as pine trees. You can find trees that lose their leaves in the fall, such as maple trees.

There are bushes and grasses, too. You will also see clover, dandelions, and colorful wildflowers. You may even find wild berries.

People plant things they want to grow in their backyard, too. You can plant an apple tree or a cherry tree. You can plant flowers. You can even grow your own vegetables.

A concept web shows all the different things that are connected to a main topic. Here we see some of the plants in a backyard habitat, both wild ones and ones people grow.

Concept Web: Plants in a Backyard Habitat

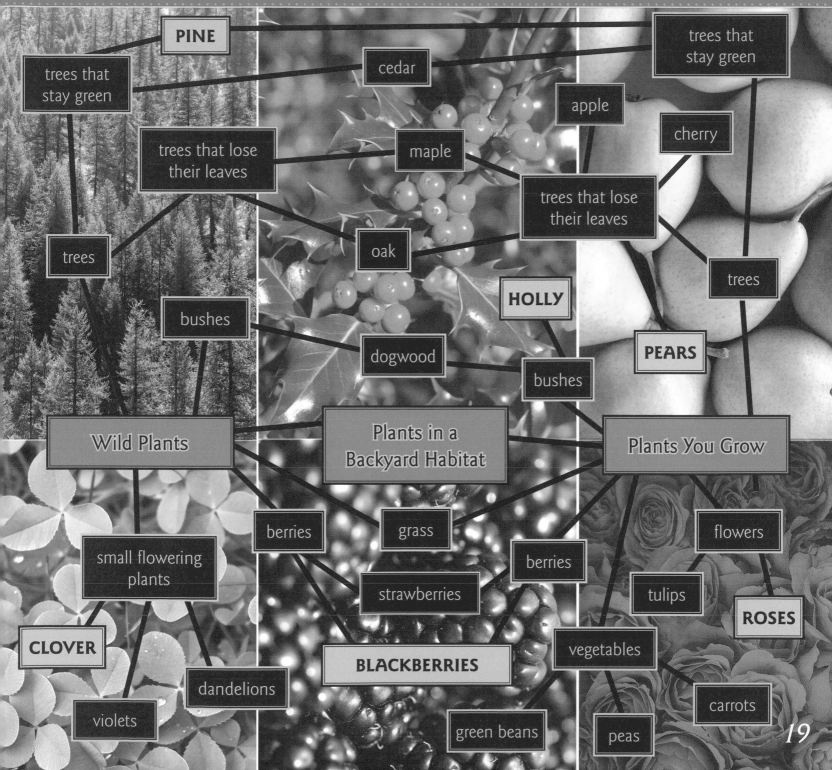

PINE

trees that stay green

trees that lose their leaves

trees

bushes

Wild Plants

small flowering plants

CLOVER

dandelions

violets

cedar

apple

maple

oak

dogwood

HOLLY

bushes

Plants in a Backyard Habitat

berries

grass

strawberries

BLACKBERRIES

green beans

trees that stay green

cherry

trees that lose their leaves

trees

PEARS

Plants You Grow

flowers

berries

tulips

ROSES

vegetables

carrots

peas

SWEET HONEYSUCKLE

Do you have a plant you like the best? Honeysuckles are popular with many people. They have beautiful flowers and dark green leaves that stay on the plant all year. These plants are so well loved that they are even named in songs.

Honeysuckles can be bushes or vines. The sweet-smelling flowers are shaped like trumpets and can be white, yellow, pink, or bright red. Inside, the flowers have sweet nectar. When the flowers fall off, berries grow.

Many animals like honeysuckles. Moths, bees, and hummingbirds like the flowers. Many birds eat the berries. Honeysuckles are perfect for a backyard habitat!

A diagram is a picture that tells you the parts that make something up. This diagram shows the parts of a honeysuckle plant.

Diagram: Honeysuckle

Stamen

Leaf

Petal

Berries

Flower

Stem

A WILDLIFE-FRIENDLY BACKYARD

Would you like to see lots of wildlife in your backyard? Here is what you need to do.

Learn what kinds of birds and animals live near you and what kinds of plants they like. Grow some of those in your backyard. Put out feeders filled with seeds for birds and squirrels. Many birds and other animals like unsalted peanuts, too. Put out special feeders with sugar water for hummingbirds and butterflies.

Now, show your friends how to make their backyards friendly for wildlife. Use what you have learned about graphic organizers to make one that shows what to do!

GLOSSARY

burrows (BUR-ohz) Holes that animals dig in the ground for shelter.

carpenter (KAHR-pen-ter) Someone who builds things with wood.

chickadees (CHIH-kuh-deez) Small birds that eat bugs, berries, and seeds.

garter snake (GAHR-ter SNAYK) A common snake with three light-colored stripes that run along the body. It does not hurt people.

goldfinches (GOHLD-finch-ez) Small, seed-eating birds with cone-shaped bills. Males are bright yellow with some black.

indigo buntings (IN-dih-goh BUN-tingz) Small, seed-eating birds with cone-shaped bills. Males are deep blue.

migrate (MY-grayt) To move from one place to another.

milk snake (MILK SNAYK) A light-colored snake with red, orange, or brown markings that have black borders. It does not hurt people.

mosquitoes (muh-SKEE-tohz) Small kinds of bugs. Females of some types will bite people and animals and suck their blood.

nectar (NEK-tur) A sweet liquid found in flowers.

newts (NOOTS) Small, brightly colored salamanders that live in or around water.

swallowtail (SWAH-loh-tayl) Describing a kind of butterfly that has a long tail on each back wing.

INDEX

WEB SITES

Due to the changing nature of Internet links, PowerKids Press has developed an online list of Web sites related to the subject of this book. This site is updated regularly. Please use this link to access the list:
www.powerkidslinks.com/graphoh/backyard/